WHO KNEW?

Other Books
by David Hoffman

The Joy of Pigging Out

*Very L.A.: The Native's Guide to
the Best of L.A.*

Kid Stuff: Great Toys from Our Childhood

WHO KNEW?

Things You Didn't Know
About Things You
Know Well

DAVID HOFFMAN

**Andrews McMeel
Publishing**

Kansas City

Library of Congress Cataloging-in-Publication Data
Hoffman, David, 1953-
    Who knew? : things you didn't know about
things you know well / by David Hoffman.
        p.   cm.
    ISBN 0-7407-0487-7 (paperback)
    1. Curiosities and wonders. 2. Handbooks,
vade-mecums, etc. I. Title.
AG243 .H65 2000
031'.02—dc21   99-55795

Book design by Holly Camerlinck

ATTENTION:
SCHOOLS AND BUSINESSES

For
Dr. Bobby

Who knew none of this, yet still managed
to know a lot

If Jell-O is hooked up to an EEG, it registers movements virtually identical to the brain waves of a healthy adult.

The original Twinkies filling was banana; it was replaced by vanilla-flavored cream during World War II, when the United States experienced a banana shortage.

On average, a Twinkie will explode in a microwave in forty-five seconds.

There are seven loops in the squiggle atop every Hostess cupcake.

There are approximately 1,750 O's in every can of SpaghettiOs.

There are 1,218 peanuts in a single twenty-eight-ounce jar of Jif peanut butter.

Peanut butter was invented by St. Louis physician Ambrose Straub, who, concerned about the nutrition of his elderly, toothless patients, concocted a health-food product that was high in protein and easily digestible.

Peanut butter's high protein content draws moisture from your mouth—which is why, in the end, it always sticks to the roof of your mouth.

One hundred shares of
McDonald's stock purchased for
$2,250 when first offered
in 1965 was worth more than
$1.4 million in 1995.

The largest McDonald's is in Beijing, China. It measures more than twenty-eight thousand square feet, seats seven hundred, and has two kitchens and twenty-nine registers.

McDonald's milkshakes contain seaweed—in the form of an extract called carrageenan, a thickener and emulsifier that keeps the butterfat in the shake from separating out.

The biggest menu flops at McDonald's include Kolacky, a Bohemian pastry that had been founder Ray Kroc's mother's specialty, and the Hula Burger, which was aimed at vegetarians (as well as Catholics who didn't eat fish on Fridays) and consisted of two slices of cheese and a grilled pineapple ring on a toasted bun.

McDonald's teaches
its employees that the
fastest way to put out a
shortening fire is to
dump frozen french fries
on it.

Some fast-food chains spray sugar on their potatoes, which caramelizes during cooking and gives the fries a golden color.

In 1853, George Crum, the head chef at Moon's Lake House in Saratoga Springs, New York, was insulted when hotel guest Cornelius Vanderbilt, the well-known railroad tycoon, sent back his dish of french fries, demanding that they be cut thinner and fried longer. In anger, Crum decided to teach the commodore a lesson and shaved off paper-thin slices of potatoes, threw them into a tub of ice water, let them soak, and dropped them into a vat of boiling grease. When they came out curled and fried crisp, he sprinkled salt on them and sent the potatoes back to the Vanderbilt table. Crum was bowled over when the guests sent back their compliments and requested another order. Soon, "Saratoga chips" (later to become simply "potato chips") were a featured item on the hotel's menu.

M&M's owe their success to the United States military, which was hungry for a candy that could hold up in G.I.s' pockets and backpacks and could be eaten without their trigger fingers getting sticky.

The original package of M&M's contained brown, yellow, orange, red, green, and violet-colored candies; violet was dropped in favor of tan in 1949. The red ones were also taken out of the mix, in 1976, but not because they contained red dye no. 2; rather, it was because company officials were afraid that customers would *think* they did.

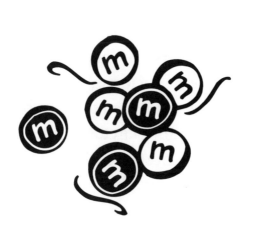

Life Savers got their signature shape by accident, when the machine employed to press out a standard circular mint malfunctioned, inadvertently punching a hole in each.

The Hershey's Kiss got its name from the puckering sound made by the manufacturing equipment as chocolate was dropped onto the conveyor belt during the production process.

Coca-Cola was first marketed as "the best cure for a hangover," and early production contained trace amounts of coca leaves, which, when processed, render cocaine.

7UP included
lithium carbonate in
its original recipe.

Dom Pérignon, the man commonly recognized for perfecting the process of both making and bottling champagne, was a Benedictine monk.

In 1891, Philadelphia inventor James Henry Mitchell revolutionized the packaged-cookie business by building an apparatus that could combine a hollow cookie crust with a fruit filling. The machinery was quickly bought by the Kennedy Biscuit Works in Boston, which had established the tradition of naming their cookies and crackers after towns in the immediate area.

Since the company already had the Beacon Hill and the Brighton, this fruit-filled number was christened the Newton. And although it was originally manufactured with a range of jam centers, fig quickly proved to be the most popular; hence the cookie officially became known as the Fig Newton.

While making cookies for her hotel guests one evening, Ruth Wakefield lacked the powdered cocoa called for in the recipe, so she substituted tiny bits of chopped chocolate in its place. Unexpectedly, the chocolate pieces did not melt in baking but, rather, held their shape, softening only slightly to a creamy texture. She served the cookies anyway, naming them Toll House after the inn she owned.

The Maxwell House was a luxury hotel in Nashville, Tennessee, known for its coffee.

In 1903, a shipload of coffee consigned to European businessman Ludwig Roselius accidentally got drenched during a storm at sea. Since the beans were no longer fit for commercial sale, Roselius used the cargo for research purposes, eventually discovering that soaking coffee beans in water was the key to decaffeination. When further experimenting proved that he could remove practically all the caffeine, but not the flavor or aroma, he decided to market his invention. He called the product Sanka, a derivation of the French phrase *sans caffeine.*

Besieged by customers' requests, Cleveland restaurant owner (and former chef at New York's Plaza Hotel) Hector Boiardi decided to bottle his famous spaghetti and meat sauce. With local success came an offer for national distribution, but, fearing that Americans would have trouble pronouncing (not to mention remembering) his Italian surname, he marketed and sold his tasty treat under the phonetic spelling, "Boy-ar-dee."

In 1880, the flour produced by Washburn, Crosby & Co., a Minnesota miller, took first place at an international exhibition held in Cincinnati. Sensing the public relations potential in their victory, company officials decided to start marketing their award-winning product under the name Gold Medal. But when an avalanche of mail poured in from housewives requesting recipes (or asking about baking problems), the men who ran Washburn, Crosby felt the responses they sent back should come from a woman. So Betty Crocker was born. The name "Betty" was picked because it was familiar and friendly; "Crocker" was chosen to honor William Crocker, a former director of the company.

At the St. Louis World's Fair in 1904, Ernest Hamwi opened up a concession to sell zalabia, a crisp, waferlike Persian pastry baked on a flat waffle iron and topped with sugar, fruit, or other sweets. The stand next to Hamwi's offered ice cream in five- and ten-cent dishes. When one day business was extremely brisk and the ice cream vendor ran out of glass cups, the quick-thinking Hamwi rolled one of his wafers into a cornucopia, let it cool, and then scooped the ice cream into its mouth. Ta-dah . . . the first ice cream cone.

The flavor we think of
as bubble gum
is a combination of
wintergreen, vanilla,
and cassia (a form of
cinnamon).

The canning process for herring
was developed in Sardinia,
which is why canned herrings
are better known as sardines.

Wedding cake was originally thrown at the bride and groom, instead of eaten by them.

A chef's hat is tall and balloons at the top so as to counteract the intense heat in the kitchen; the unique shape allows air to circulate around the scalp, keeping the head cool.

Before attending the Cordon Bleu, before mastering the art of French cooking, Julia Child did intelligence work for the Office of Strategic Services in India and China during World War II.

The five interlocking Olympic rings are black, blue, red, white, and yellow because at least one of these colors appears on every national flag.

One of the highest-priced single purchases ever charged to an American Express card was $2.5 million—for a painting by Roy Lichtenstein.

The original American
Express card was purple
(and was for eleven
years, until the
green card replaced it
in 1969).

Banks are commonly shaped
like pigs because in the
eighteenth century frugal
people saved their money in
earthenware jars made of dense
orange clay known as pygg.

The dollar sign is a combination of the letters P and S, PS being the abbreviation for pesos, the principal coin in circulation in the United States until 1794, when we began marketing our own dollars.

The paper used to make money is composed of linen and several types of cotton, including denim—which gives it its unique fabriclike feel and durability.

Most American currency contains microprinted messages to prevent counterfeiting:

On the one-dollar bill, there is an owl in the upper left-hand corner of the "1" and a spider hidden at the upper right.

The phrase "United States of America" is camouflaged within the lapel of Benjamin Franklin's jacket on the newer one-hundred-dollar bill.

The same twenty-six states engraved across the top of the actual Lincoln Memorial are listed atop the image of the Memorial seen on the back of the five dollar bill.

A dime has 118 ridges around the edge.

A portrait of Franklin Delano Roosevelt appears on the dime because of his work on behalf of the March of Dimes and its battle against polio, the disease that crippled him.

Three of the first five
U.S. Presidents—
John Adams, Thomas
Jefferson, and James
Monroe—died on
July 4th.

James Madison, the fourth
President of the United States,
stood only five feet four inches
tall and weighed less than
one hundred pounds.

When the gray exterior of the
Presidential Mansion was
painted white to cover the fire
damage caused by British Forces
in the War of 1812, the change
in color brought along a change
in name: the White House.

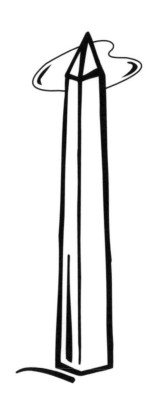

There is a subtle change in color in the Washington Monument about one-third of the way up, because during the construction process builders changed materials—from Maryland marble to Massachusetts marble.

The Pentagon, one of the largest office buildings in the world, has twice as many bathrooms as is necessary, because when it was built Virginia laws still required separate toilet facilities for blacks and whites.

While his wife spent long hours posing for the figure, the model for the face of the Statue of Liberty was Charlotte Bartholdi, mother of the French sculptor Frédéric-Auguste Bartholdi, who designed it.

Portrait artist James Whistler decided to paint his mother when the person who had scheduled an appointment with him failed to show.

The man who
commissioned the
Mona Lisa refused it.

Big Ben is not a clock,
but the thirteen-ton bell
inside the clock tower
of England's House
of Parliament.

The flashing warning light atop
the Capitol Records Tower
in Hollywood also spells out
H-O-L-L-Y-W-O-O-D
in Morse code.

In 1899, pharmacist George Bunting blended his own cold cream, which, in addition to removing makeup and relieving sunburn, gained popularity for its ability to cure eczema. The "No Eczema" claim not only became the product's major selling point, it also gave it its name: Noxzema.

Sunglasses date back to
fifteenth-century China,
where they were worn by
judges to conceal their
expressions while presiding
over court.

The idea of painting fingernails originated in China, where the color of someone's nails indicated their social rank.

"Avon" comes from Stratford-on-Avon, since it was volumes of Shakespeare that company founder David McConnell first sold door-to-door. However, when the complimentary vial of perfume he gave to each housewife proved more popular than the books, a cosmetics company was born.

The first piece of Tupperware was a bathroom tumbler— and was sold only in department stores.

The kitchen dishwasher was invented by the socialite wife of an Illinois politician, not because she was fed up with the ho-hum chore of dirty dishes but because she had had it with careless servants who too frequently broke her expensive china while washing it.

The microwave was born when an engineer testing a magnetron tube noticed that the radiation leaking from it had caused the chocolate bar in his pocket to melt.

Following the sales success of his disposable ballpoint pen in Europe, French businessman Marcel Bich was ready to take on the international market. He had named the product after himself, but realizing that Americans would incorrectly pronounce the name (spelled Bich) as *bitch*, he smartly dropped the H and called his pen Bic.

A book of maps is called an atlas because early editions commonly featured a picture of Atlas, carrying the world on his shoulders, on the cover.

According to author L. Frank
Baum, the name Oz was
thought up when he looked at
his filing cabinet and noticed
one drawer marked A–G,
a second tagged H–N, and
a third labeled O–Z.

Erich Segal, the author of *Love Story,* was one of the screenwriters of *Yellow Submarine.*

"Cinderella" has been made into a movie more times than any other story.

From Russia with Love was chosen as the second James Bond novel to be adapted as a film after President John Kennedy listed it as one of his ten favorite books of all time.

The computer in *2001: A Space Odyssey* was called HAL as a tongue-in-cheek reference to IBM. The name was derived from the fact that the letters H-A-L precede the letters I-B-M in the alphabet.

To make things easier while mixing the
American Graffiti sound track, George
Lucas and sound designer Walter Murch
labeled all of the reels of film R and all
of the dialogue tracks D, and then
numbered each of them sequentially,
starting with 1. When Murch later
asked Lucas for Reel 2, Dialogue 2—or
more precisely, R2, D2—Lucas liked the
way it sounded so much that he made a
note of the name for another project
he was writing.

It was the sight of Clark Gable peeling a raw carrot with a penknife, then munching on it (as he attempted to teach Claudette Colbert how to hitchhike) in *It Happened One Night* that inspired Warner Brothers animator Bob Clampett to give Bugs Bunny his signature carrot chomp.

The sight of oranges in all three *Godfather* films signals that death (or a close call) is about to happen.

Director Wes Craven named Freddy Krueger after a kid who bullied him in school.

Peter Sellers modeled his portrayal of Inspector Clouseau—particularly the mustache and the proud stance—after Captain Matthew Webb, the first person to swim the English Channel.

Neil Simon's *The Goodbye Girl* began life as *Bogart Slept Here* (changed from the first title, *Gable Slept Here*) and was based on Dustin Hoffman's life as a struggling actor prior to *The Graduate*.

In *The Graduate,* the parts of Benjamin Braddock and Mrs. Robinson (Anne Bancroft) were originally offered to Robert Redford and Doris Day.

Burt Reynolds was cast as Han Solo in *Star Wars*, but dropped out before filming began.

The title role in
Beetlejuice was written
for Sammy Davis Jr.

All of the still photos of
Forrest Gump picture
him with his eyes closed.

According to the film's animators, you'll see 6,469,952 black spots every time you watch *101 Dalmatians*.

In *Pulp Fiction*, the word
f**k is used 257 times.

22 cigarettes are smoked
in *Casablanca*

Because the studio expected it to bomb, the budget of *Casablanca* was so low that the plane used in the background of the final scene was a small cardboard cutout. To give it the illusion of being full-sized, the producers hired midgets to portray the crew preparing it for takeoff.

Despite its 216-minute running time, *Lawrence of Arabia* has no women in speaking roles.

Marilyn Monroe developed her signature walk by hacking off the heel of one shoe.

Oscar winner Tommy Lee Jones was the college roommate (Harvard, class of 1969) of Vice President Al Gore.

When the name Alan Smithee
is credited as a film's director
it means that the real director
has disavowed the project and
does not want his or her
real name to be used.

Annie Hall was originally written and shot as a murder mystery, but during postproduction Woody Allen realized that the strongest footage was of the relationship between the two main characters, so the film was pared down and reedited as a romantic comedy.

The signature line drawing of Alfred Hitchcock's profile was drawn by Alfred Hitchcock.

Hitchcock purchased the film rights to Robert Bloch's novel *Psycho* anonymously—and then proceeded to buy up as many copies of the book as he could in order to keep the ending a secret.

The stabbing sound the knife makes in the shower scene in *Psycho* is in fact the sound of a knife stabbing a melon.

A recording of a camel's moan was slowed down and used as the sound of the tornado in *Twister.*

Houseflies hum
in the key of F.

WHO KNEW

Cats have two sets of
vocal chords.

Tigers have striped skin,
not just striped fur.

The Venus flytrap feeds
primarily on ants,
not flies.

The female praying
mantis chews her
partner's head off
during mating.

118

Each instance of dog poop that goes unscooped attracts approximately 144 flies.

The number of cricket chirps
you count in a fifteen-second
interval, plus thirty-seven,
will tell you the current
air temperature.

Bulls are color-blind and cannot see red. It is the bright color and motion of the cape that causes them to charge.

Bullwhips, when properly snapped, exceed speeds of 742 miles per hour, thus breaking the sound barrier.

The ostrich cannot fly,
but it can outrun
a racehorse.

An ostrich's eye is bigger than its brain.

The original Volkswagen Beetle was commissioned by Adolf Hitler and designed by Ferdinand Porsche.

In the early 1920s, taxicab company owner John Hertz (who would later go on to start a rental car business) funded a University of Chicago study to determine which color in the spectrum was most visible from a far distance. When the answer came back "yellow," he had all of the cars in his fleet painted exactly that, beginning a tradition that would catch on nationwide, and carry over to school buses and traffic signs.

The name Jeep is derivative
of the expression "G.P.,"
military slang for
General Purpose Vehicle.

The name Nike emanates from Greek mythology; appropriately, she was the winged goddess of victory.

The company's famed swoosh logo was purchased from the portfolio of a student at Portland State—for thirty-five dollars. The design was purposefully created and positioned to not only serve as a product ID but also to give the shoe additional lateral support.

Nike's signature design came when a former runner at the University of Oregon and his college coach, in an attempt to build a better, lighter sneaker, took a piece of rubber, stuck it into a waffle iron, and crafted a crisscross-patterned sole that markedly increased traction.

When G. H. Bass introduced a casual slip-on loafer based on one being manufactured and worn in Oslo, he paid tribute to the shoe's Norwegian roots and called his version Weejuns.

Panama hats are actually made in Ecuador.

The Beach Boys toyed with calling themselves the Pendletons, figuring that if they did they would get free shirts.

When former chicken-plucker-turned-singer Ernest Evans decided to change his name, he chose Chubby Checker to honor his idol, Fats Domino.

Among the 437 "folk and roll singers" who answered the 1965 audition call to be a Monkee were Stephen Stills (who was rejected because he had bad teeth and a receding hairline), Harry Nilsson, and Paul Williams.

Two years later, when the group went out on their first concert tour, their nonbilled opening act was Jimi Hendrix.

Because of Davy Jones's huge popularity as a member of The Monkees, another young singer in London, also named David Jones, was forced to change his name . . . to David Bowie.

The jukebox got its name from *jook*, African-American slang for "dance."

Kemo sabe means "white shirt" in Apache.

Tip is an acronym for "to insure promptness"— and once upon a time was given in advance.

The word *news* was coined from the fact that early daily papers carried images of globes on their mastheads and boasted that their reports came from all directions—North, East, West, and South.

X's symbolize kisses because in ancient days, when few people knew how to write, they would simply sign an X to show their agreement, then kiss the mark to emphasize their sincerity.

The phrase *hanky panky* stems from the magician's practice of using a handkerchief in one hand to distract the audience from noticing what he is doing with the other.

No word in the English language rhymes with month, orange, silver, or purple.

The only word in the English language with five vowels in a row is *queueing,* unless you spell meow "m-i-a-o-u" (as some dictionaries do), in which case *miaouing* also has five.

Stewardesses is the longest word that is typed using only the left hand.

Maine is the only state whose name is just one syllable.

There are portions of Wisconsin that are farther east than parts of Florida.

Podunk is in
Massachusetts.

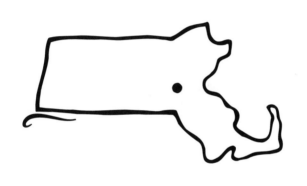

In terms of area, Juneau, Alaska, is the largest city in the United States, yet it can only be reached by boat or plane.

There is a regulation-size half-court on which employees can play basketball inside the Matterhorn at Disneyland.

The gold decorating the exterior
of It's a Small World at
Disneyland isn't paint but,
in fact, twenty-four-karat
gold leaf.

When Disneyland opened in 1955, Tomorrowland represented a city from 1986.

An unbelievably rude waiter at Oscar's Tavern in New York so unintentionally amused Muppet creator Jim Henson and *Sesame Street* director Jon Stone that he inspired the creation of Oscar the Grouch.

Bert and Ernie are believed to be named after Bert the cop and Ernie the taxi driver in *It's a Wonderful Life.*

Big Bird's costume is
made of turkey feathers,
dyed yellow.

The original Clarabelle in *Howdy Doody* was played by Bob Keeshan, who went on to become Captain Kangaroo. The first Ronald McDonald was *Today* show personality Willard Scott.

The three-tone musical chime that identifies NBC is composed of three notes—G, E, and C—which is short for the company's original (and now current) owner, General Electric Corporation.

Seinfeld wasn't Jerry Seinfeld's first sitcom. He played the governor's speechwriter on *Benson,* but was fired after three episodes.

The coffee shop frequented by Jerry, George, Elaine, and Kramer was called Monk's because there was a Thelonious Monk poster in the office where Seinfeld and cocreator Larry David would write.

The Mod Squad was
based on a true story.

In most TV commercials and print advertisements, the hands on a watch are set at 10:10 because that arrangement draws attention to the logo and frames the manufacturer's name.

Aunt Harriet, the matriarch of stately Wayne mansion, never existed in the comic-book version of *Batman* but was created specifically for the TV series because producers feared that two bachelors (and a butler!) living together had homosexual overtones.

Ralph Kramden's address in *The Honeymooners*—328 Chauncey Street—was actually the real address of Jackie Gleason's childhood home.

The X-Files's Detective Scully was named in honor of Vin Scully, the well-loved announcer for the Los Angeles Dodgers. "Mulder" for the record, is show creator Chris Carter's mother's maiden name.

On *Happy Days,* creator Garry Marshall originally planned to call the motorcycle-riding tough guy Arthur Masciarelli, which is his real life family surname. But that made the character's nickname Mash; since there was already a successful book, movie, and TV series known as that, Masciarelli became Fonzarelli, and Henry Winkler became the Fonz.

Bullwinkle was the name
of a car dealership in
Oakland, California.

June Foray, the voice of Rocky, the flying squirrel, was also the voice of the Chatty Cathy doll.

Barbie's last name is
Roberts.

A standard-size Slinky
comprises eighty feet
of wire.

Lincoln Logs were invented by John Lloyd Wright, the son of Frank Lloyd Wright. He got the idea from a building technique his father had used in designing Tokyo's Imperial Hotel.

Silly Putty resulted from a failed World War II effort to develop an inexpensive synthetic substitute for rubber.

Play-Doh was originally formulated as a compound to clean wallpaper.

The ingredient believed to give the clay its unique smell is vanilla.

The smell of Crayola crayons is so familiar that it is one of the twenty most recognizable scents to American adults (ranking up there with coffee and peanut butter) and so soothing that sniffing them has been proven to lower blood pressure.

In the 1970s, in order to stop kids from sniffing airplane glue, the manufacturers added an intense oil of mustard to the formula.

The total amount of money in a standard Monopoly game is $15,140; real money was slipped into packs of play money that were smuggled into POW camps inside Germany during World War II.

The fifty-two playing cards
in a typical deck represent
the fifty-two weeks in a year;
the four suits, the four seasons.

Six eight-stud Lego
pieces can be combined
102,981,500 ways.

The Rubik's Cube can be twisted and turned into over forty-three quintillion (43,252,003,274,489,856,000, to be exact) configurations in the attempt to line up one solid color on all six sides.

Mexican jumping beans jump because there is an actual one-quarter-inch caterpillar trapped inside.

The liquid inside a Magic 8-Ball consists of water, blue coloring, and propylene glycol, an antifreeze to keep the solution from turning solid during shipping.

The Ouija board
got its name from the
combination of the
French and German
words for "yes"—
oui and *ja*.

The name Atari was chosen so that consumers would think that the Northern California–based company was Japanese.

Despite repeated requests for Elvis, the only real people ever depicted as Pez dispensers have been Betsy Ross and Daniel Boone.

Donald Duncan—of Duncan Yo-Yo fame—was also responsible for marketing the first parking meters.

The nail on both thumbs of
every G.I. Joe is deliberately cast
on the inside (as opposed to the
outside) of the hand so as to give
the action figure an easily
identifiable characteristic that
doubles as a trademark.

On the average, we
forget 80 percent of
what we learn
on any given day.

Photograph by Steven Schatzberg

David Hoffman is the author of the best-selling books *The Joy of Pigging Out* and *Kid Stuff*. He has worked in television for twenty years, as both a series writer and on-camera reporter covering trends and popular culture. He lives in Los Angeles.

Trademark Acknowledgments

Jell-O is a trademark of Kraft Foods Inc.

Twinkies and Hostess are trademarks of Continental Baking Company.

SpaghettiOs and Chef Boyardee are trademarks of American Home Food Products.

Jif is a trademark of Procter & Gamble Company.

McDonald's and Ronald McDonald are trademarks of McDonald's Corporation.

M&M's is a trademark of Mars Inc.

LifeSavers is a trademark of Nabisco Inc.

Hershey's Kiss is a trademark of Hershey Foods Corporation.

Coca-Cola is a trademark of the Coca-Cola Company.

7UP is a trademark of the Dr. Pepper/Seven-Up Corporation.

Dom Pérignon is a trademark of Schieffelin & Company.

Toll House is a trademark of Societe de Produits Nestlé S.A.

Maxwell House is a trademark of Kraft Foods Inc.

Sanka is a trademark of Societe Anonyme Fabriques de Produits de Chimie Organique de Laire.

Fig Newtons is a trademark of National Biscuit Company.

Gold Medal and Betty Crocker are trademarks of General Mills Inc.

American Express is a trademark of American Express Company.

Capitol Records Tower is a trademark of Capitol Records Inc.

Noxzema is a trademark of Noxell Corporation.

Avon is a trademark of Avon Products Inc.

Tupperware is a trademark of Dart Industries Inc.

Bic is a trademark of BIC Corporation.

Oz is a trademark of Turner Entertainment Company.

Freddy Krueger is a trademark of New Line Cinema Corporation.

Forrest Gump is a trademark of Paramount Pictures Corporation.

Volkswagen Beetle is a trademark of Volkswagen Aktiengesellschaft.